Hal Leonard Student Piano Library

Piano Lessons

Book 4

FOREWORD

When music excites our interest and imagination, we eagerly put our hearts into learning it. The music in the **Hal Leonard Student Piano Library** encourages practice, progress, confidence, and best of all – success! Over 1,000 students and teachers in a nationwide test market responded with enthusiasm to the:

- variety of styles and moods
- natural rhythmic flow, singable melodies and lyrics
- "best ever" teacher accompaniments
- improvisations integrated throughout the **Lesson Books**
- instrumental accompaniments to every piece available on the students' very own CD or General MIDI Disk.

When new concepts have an immediate application to the music, the effort it takes to learn these skills seems worth it. Test market teachers and students were especially excited about the:

- "realistic" pacing that challenges without overwhelming
- clear and concise presentation of concepts that allows room for a teacher's individual approach
- uncluttered page layout that keeps the focus on the music.

In addition, the **Piano Practice Games** books present basic theory, technique and creativity in ways that relate directly to the music in the **Lesson Books**. The **Piano Solos** series reinforces concepts with challenging performance repertoire.

The **Hal Leonard Student Piano Library** is the result of the efforts of many individuals. We extend our gratitude to all the teachers, students and colleagues who shared their energy and creative input. May this method guide your learning as you bring this music to life.

Best wishes,

Barbara Kreader   Fred Kern   Phillip Keveren

Authors
**Barbara Kreader, Fred Kern,
Phillip Keveren**

Consultants
Mona Rejino, Tony Caramia,
Bruce Berr, Richard Rejino

*Director,
Educational Keyboard Publications*
Margaret Otwell

Editor
Carol Klose

Illustrator
Fred Bell

Book: ISBN 0-7935-7690-3
Book/CD: ISBN 0-634-03121-X

HAL•LEONARD®
CORPORATION

7777 W. BLUEMOUND RD. P.O. BOX 13819 MILWAUKEE, WI 53213

Visit Hal Leonard Online at
www.halleonard.com

REVIEW OF BOOK THREE

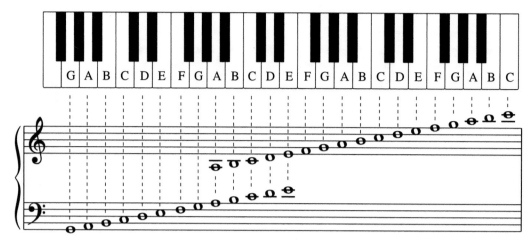

NOTE VALUES

eighth notes
two eighth notes fill the
time of one quarter note

dotted-quarter eighth pattern
fills the time of two quarter notes

INTERVALS

Interval of a 6th

half step
the distance from one key to
another, with no key in between

whole step
the distance from one key to
another, with one key in between

FIVE-FINGER PATTERNS

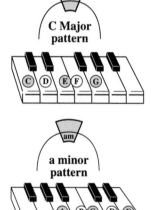

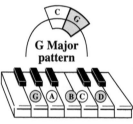

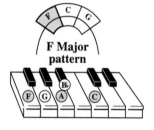

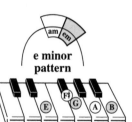

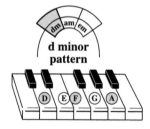

MUSICAL TERMS

time signature $\frac{2}{4}$	two beats fill every measure quarter note gets one beat
loco	play the notes where written
a tempo	return to the original tempo
D.S. (Dal Segno) al Fine	return to 𝄋 (*segno*) and play to the end (*fine*)
D.C. (Da Capo) al Coda	return to the beginning and play to the first coda sign ⊕ ; then skip to the next coda sign ⊕
15ma	play two octaves higher than written

CONTENTS

* Students can check pieces as they play them.

Related Five-Finger Patterns

Every major five-finger pattern has a related minor five-finger pattern.

To find the related minor pattern:
1. Play the major pattern with your L.H.
2. Place your R.H. thumb one whole step above the highest note of the major pattern.
3. Play the minor pattern with your R.H.

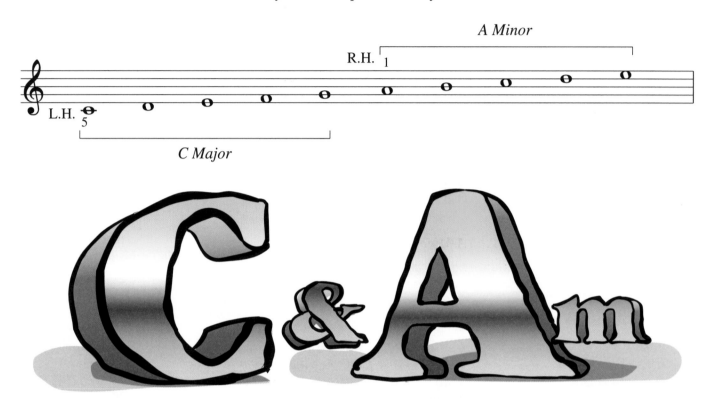

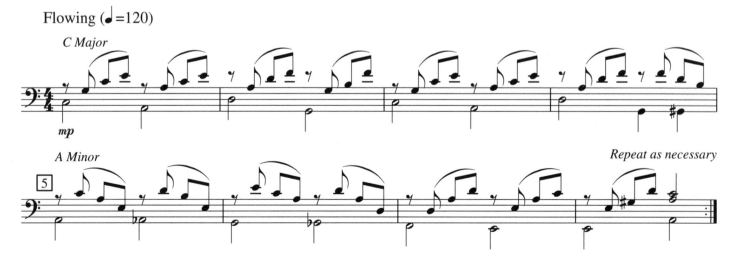

My Own Song
in C Major & A Minor

As you listen to the accompaniment, improvise a melody using the **C Major** pattern with your L.H. and the **A Minor** pattern (relative minor) with your R.H. Begin playing in the C Major pattern. Your teacher will tell you when to change to the A Minor pattern.

Accompaniment (Student improvises one octave higher than shown above.)

Rustic Dance

Barbara Kreader

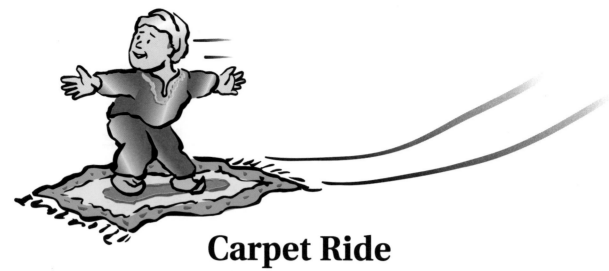

Carpet Ride

Mysteriously (♩=135) 4/5 3

Phillip Keveren

Cross 2 over 1

My Own Song
in G Major & E Minor

As you listen to the accompaniment, improvise a melody using the **G Major** pattern with your
L.H. and the **E Minor** pattern (relative minor) with your R.H. Begin playing in the G Major pattern.
Your teacher will tell you when to change to the E Minor pattern.

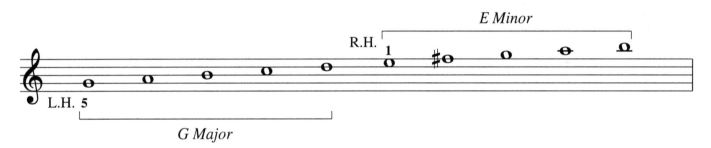

Accompaniment (Student improvises one octave higher than shown above.)

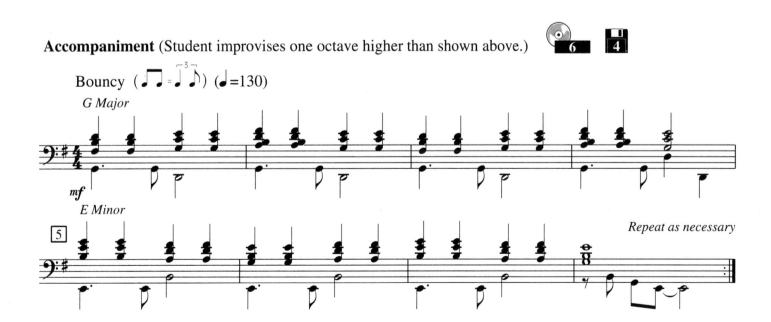

Clap and count these patterns:

Mister Banjo

Creole
Arranged by Phillip Keveren

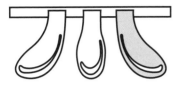

SYNCOPATED PEDALING

When you press the damper pedal, the tones will continue to ring after you release the keys. To produce a smooth sound, release and press the pedal quickly. Always keep your heel on the floor.

Change the damper pedal **immediately after** playing the notes. Pedaling too late will cause the sound to blur; pedaling too early will cause a break in the sound.

Morning Bells

With energy ($\bullet$=135) 9/10 6

Phillip Keveren

Press down   hold   release and press down

Press down and let the bells ring!

9

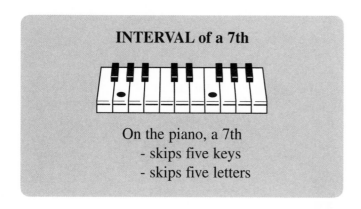

INTERVAL of a 7th

On the piano, a 7th
- skips five keys
- skips five letters

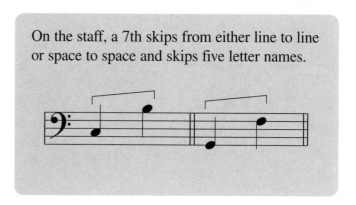

On the staff, a 7th skips from either line to line or space to space and skips five letter names.

Ribbons

Smoothly (♩=95)

Fred Kern

MAJOR SCALE PATTERNS

All **Major Scale Patterns** are made up of eight tones
in the following order of half steps and whole steps.

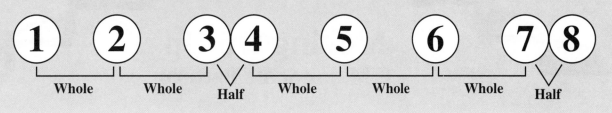

C Major Scale

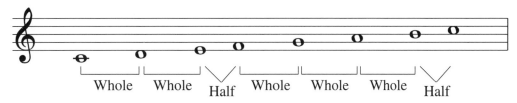

Scale Preparation

Prepare to play a scale by first practicing the thumb movements.
Let your arm guide your fingers smoothly up and down the keyboard.

* Allegretto

Katherine Glaser

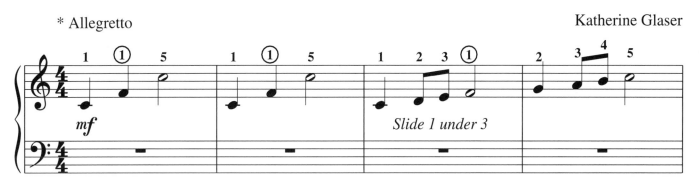

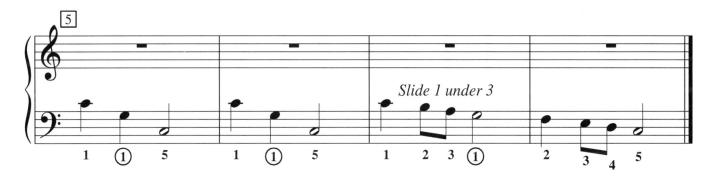

Accompaniment (Student plays one octave higher.)

Allegretto (♩=120)

* *Allegretto means quickly, but not as fast as allegro.*

11

Moving On Up
C Major Scale Pattern

Accompaniment (Student plays two octaves higher than written.)

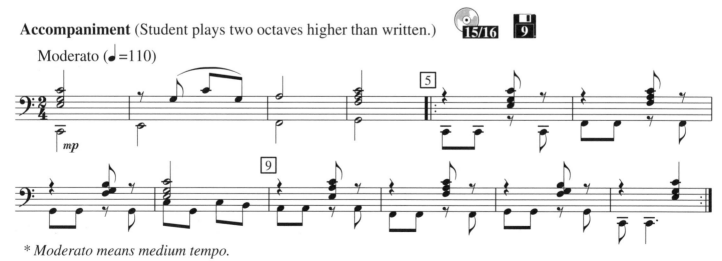

* *Moderato means medium tempo.*

Calypso Cat

Key of C Major

Key signature: *no sharps, no flats*

Happily (♩=140)

Phillip Keveren

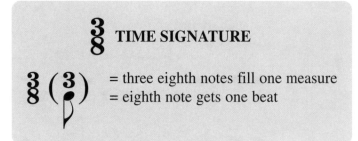

Jig

Irish
Arranged by Fred Kern

14

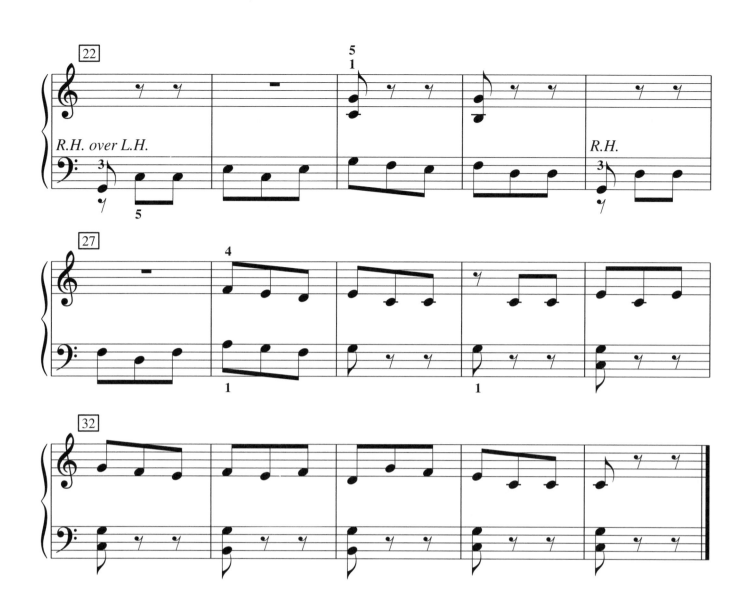

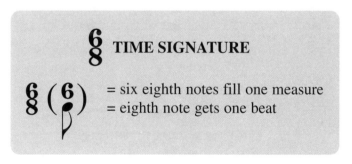

$\frac{6}{8}$ **TIME SIGNATURE**

$\frac{6}{8}$ $\left(\frac{6}{\text{♪}}\right)$ = six eighth notes fill one measure
= eighth note gets one beat

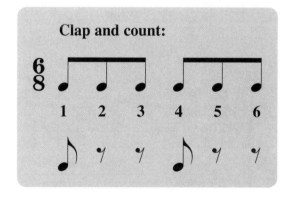

Clap and count:

ACCIDENTALS

Sharps (♯), Flats (♭) or Naturals (♮) added to a piece outside the key signature are called **Accidentals**.

Clap and count these patterns:

Two-Four-Six-Eight

Jazzy (♩.=93) **21/22** **12**

Bill Boyd

Relative Scales

Every Major Scale has a Relative Minor. It begins on the sixth step of the major scale.

A is the sixth tone of the C Major scale. C Major and A Minor are **Relative Scales** because they have the same **Key Signature:** *no sharps and no flats.*

C Major Scale

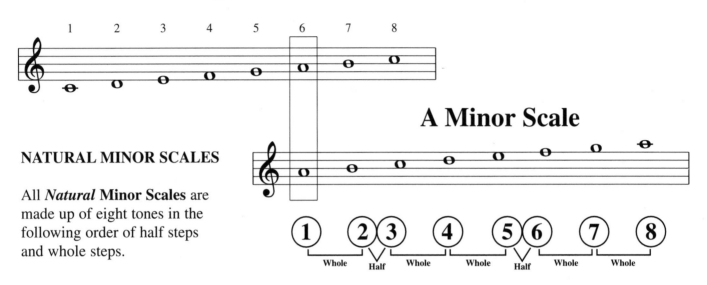

NATURAL MINOR SCALES

All *Natural* Minor Scales are made up of eight tones in the following order of half steps and whole steps.

HARMONIC MINOR SCALES

The *Harmonic* form of the minor scale raises the seventh tone one half step indicated by an accidental. The A Harmonic Minor Scale has a G♯.

For a quick way to find the relative minor,
move down 3 half steps from the first tone of the major scale.

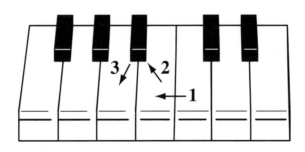

"A" is 3 half steps below "C".

Moving On Up
A Minor Scale Patterns

First, play the *Natural Minor Scale* with no sharps.
On the repeat, play the *Harmonic Minor Scale* with the raised 7th (G♯).

Accompaniment (Student plays two octaves higher than written.)

First, play the natural form with no sharps or flats.
On the repeat, play the harmonic form with the raised 7th (G♯).

Moderato (♩=110)

Allegro

Key of A Minor

Key signature: _____

Cornelius Gurlitt
(1820-1901)
Op. 82, No. 52

*Etude

Key of A Minor

Key signature: _____

Ludwig Schytte
(1848-1909)

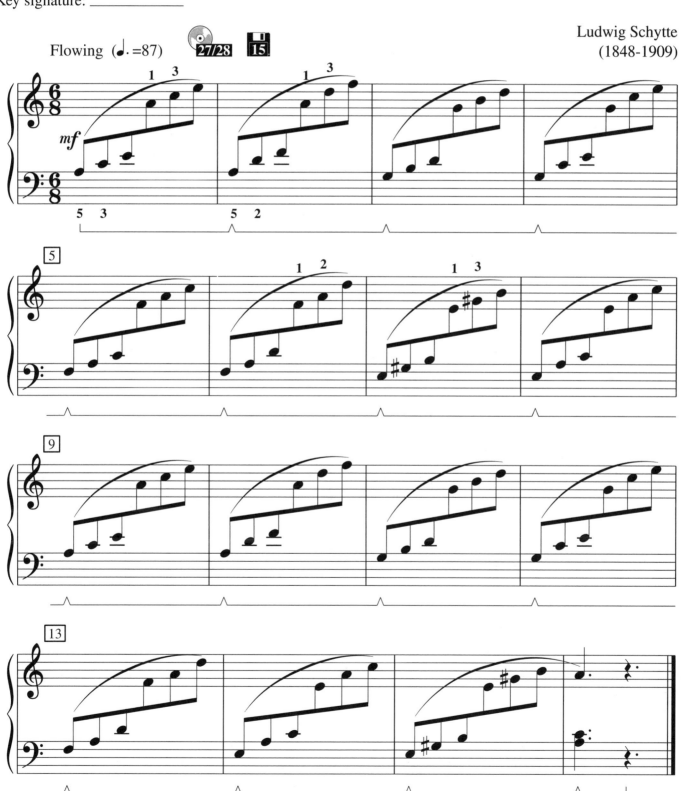

*Etude means a study or exercise piece.

TRIADS IN ROOT POSITION

Root Position Triads can be built on any tone of the scale and are written on three lines or three spaces.

PRIMARY TRIADS

Chords built on the 1st, 4th and 5th tones of the scale are called **Primary Triads: Tonic (I)**, **Sub-dominant (IV)**, **Dominant (V)**.

The Primary Triads in C Major are:

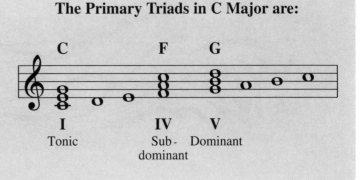

Take It Easy
Chord warm-up in root position

Phillip Keveren

Teacher Solo (Play one octave higher than written.) **29/30** **16**

22

The **G7 chord** includes F,
the 7th tone above G.

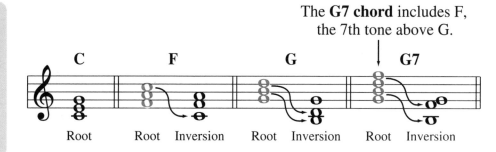

Root   Root   Inversion   Root   Inversion   Root   Inversion

Close By
Chord warm-up in close position

Phillip Keveren

Teacher Solo (Student plays two octaves higher than written.)

Flowing ($\quarternote$=135)

My Own Song   **Improvisation using *C Major Triads***

As your teacher plays the student part to *Close By,* improvise a new melody in the key of **C Major**.

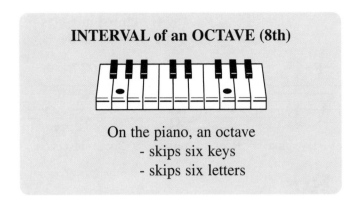
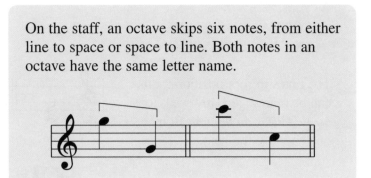
Jumping Beans

Allegro *giocoso ($\quarternote$ =165)   34/35   1 19   Kreader, Kern, Keveren

* *Giocoso means humorous*

24

Relay Race

Carl Czerny
(1791-1857)

The Primary Triads in **A Minor** are:

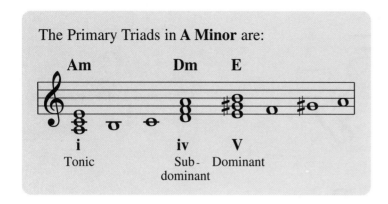

i — Tonic
iv — Sub-dominant
V — Dominant

Practice these chords in **close position** before playing *A Minor Tango*:

The **E7 chord** includes D, the 7th tone above E.

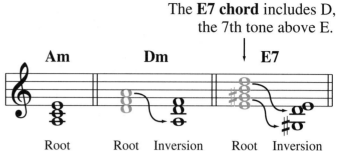

Root   Root   Inversion   Root   Inversion

A Minor Tango

Moderato

Phillip Keveren

Teacher Solo

Moderato (♩=120)   38/39   21

My Own Song   **Improvisation using *A Minor Triads***   40   22

As your teacher plays the student part to *A Minor Tango*, improvise a new melody in the key of **A Minor**.

All The Pretty Little Horses

American
Arranged by Fred Kern

Joshua Fit The Battle Of Jericho

Theme and Variations

Theme: **Traditional**
Allegretto (♩=170)

Phillip Keveren

Variation I: **Classical**
Fleeting (♩=185) *1st time both hands 8va*

28

Variation II: Swing

Laid-back Jazz (♩=150)

G Major Scale Pattern

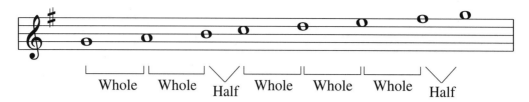

Whole   Whole   Half   Whole   Whole   Whole   Half

Moving On Up

Key of G Major
Key signature: *one sharp, F♯*

Accompaniment (Student plays one octave higher than written.) 45/46 25

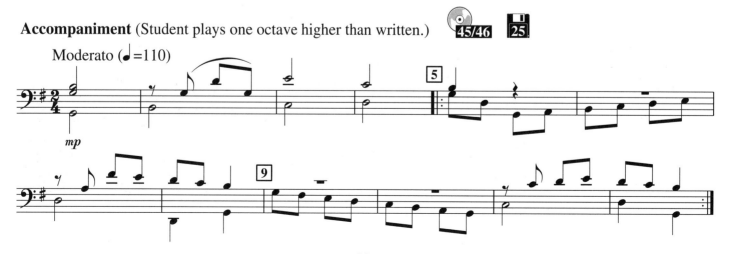

Spanish Dance

Key of G Major

Key signature: _____

Muzio Clementi
(1752-1832)
Adapted by Fred Kern

* Vivace means lively.

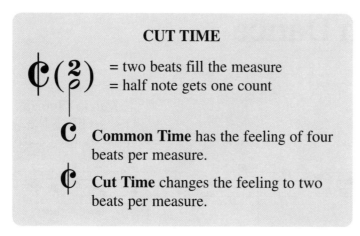

Clap and count these patterns:

True Blues

Slowly (♩=60)   49/50   27

Bill Boyd

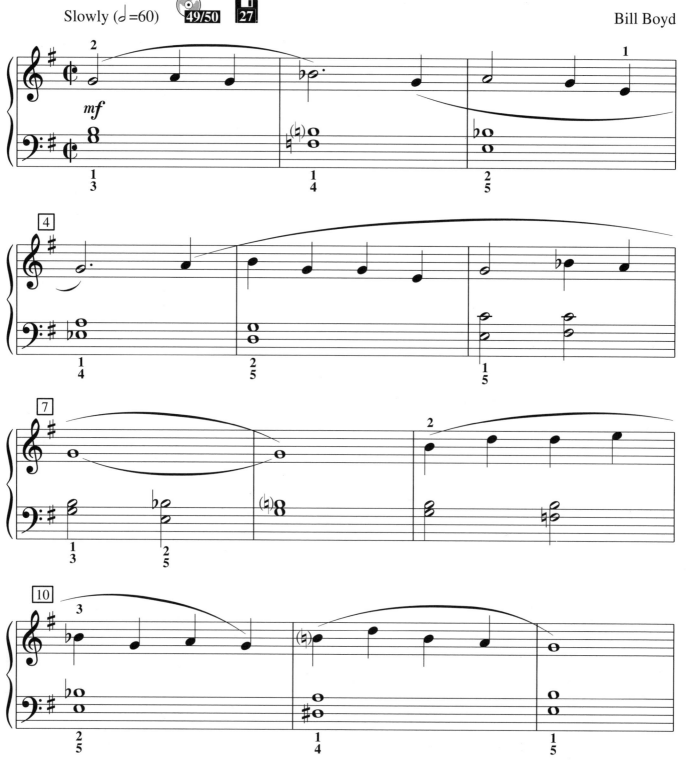

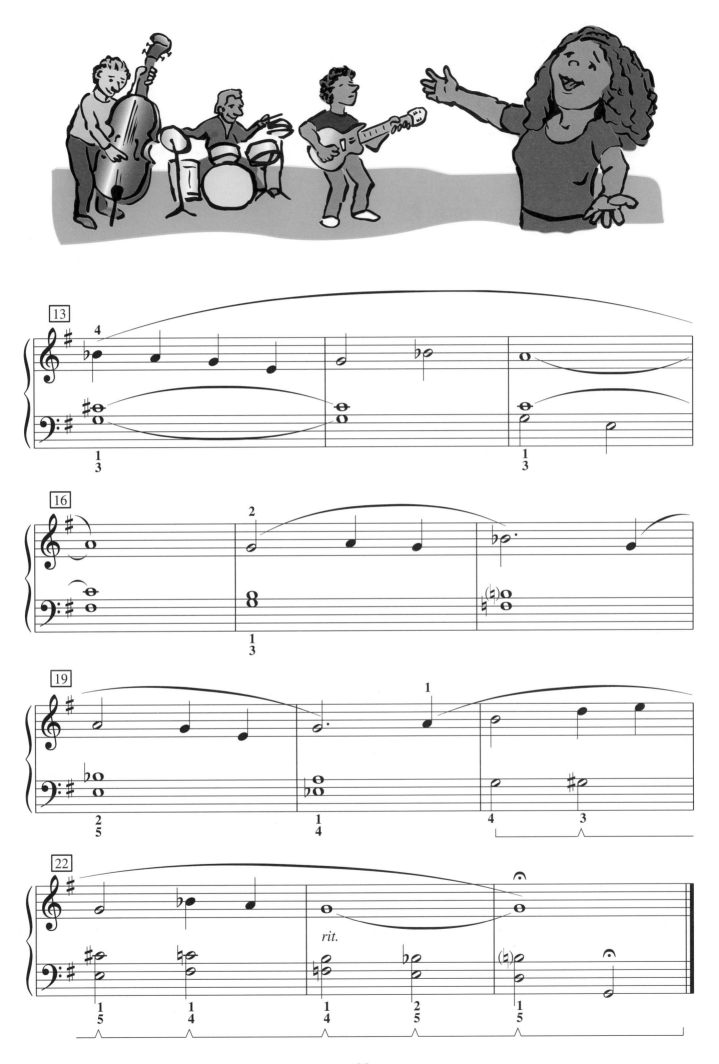

TRIPLETS

An eighth note **Triplet** fills the time of one quarter note.

Blues For A Count

Moving along (♩=120)

Bruce Berr

Clap and count these patterns:

Doo Wop Ditty

Happily, in no big hurry (♩=65)

Phillip Keveren

E Minor Scale Patterns
Natural Minor

The *Harmonic Minor Scale* raises the seventh tone one half step (D♯).

Moving On Up

Key of E Minor
Key signature: *one sharp, F♯*

First, play the *Natural Minor Scale* with the F♯.
On the repeat, play the *Harmonic Minor Scale* with the raised 7th (D♯).

Moderato

Accompaniment (Student plays one octave higher than written.) 55/56 30

First, play the natural form with F♯.
On the repeat, play the harmonic form with the raised 7th (D♯).

Moderato (♩=110)